This book belongs to

_____

_____

and I am finding out
about the story
of Easter

Easter is nearly here.
It's celebrated all over the world!

People send Easter cards
decorated with bunnies and chicks.
They give each other presents
and lots of chocolate.

But why do we celebrate?
What's the true meaning of Easter?

This little book retells the story
of the very first Easter
– and why it still matters for us.

Would you like to know
The Story of
Easter?

by Tim Dowley
Illustrated by Eira Reeves

CANDLE
BOOKS

Jesus was going to a great feast
in Jerusalem.

He took with him his twelve special friends, the twelve disciples.

Jesus borrowed a donkey
and rode into the city.

People threw palm branches on the road. "Hosanna!" they shouted. "Hooray for God!"

Jesus ate a special supper with his friends in an upstairs room.

He gave them bread and wine.
He knew he was going to die soon.

But one man sneaked out. His name was Judas, and he was plotting against Jesus.

After supper, Jesus took his friends
to pray in a garden outside the city.

While Jesus was praying, they all fell asleep.

Suddenly Judas appeared with soldiers.

They marched Jesus to the ruler, Pilate.

"Jesus is making trouble," people shouted. "Kill him! Kill him!"

So Pilate sent Jesus to die on a hill outside the city. Soldiers put Jesus on a wooden cross.

"Father, forgive them!" he prayed.
The sky went dark. Jesus died.

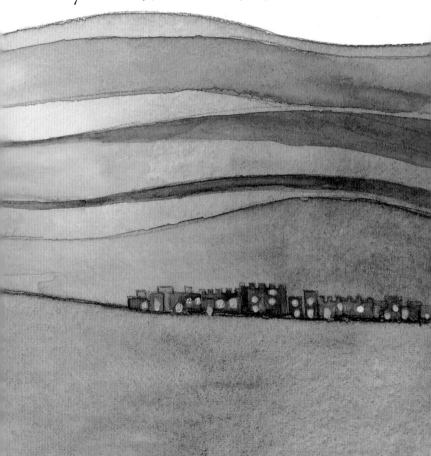

Jesus' family and friends watched
very sadly.

A good man laid Jesus' body in a tomb.
He rolled a great stone across the door.

Early Sunday morning, some women went to Jesus' tomb.

The stone was rolled away!

Suddenly two angels stood there.
"Jesus is risen from the dead!" they said.

The women ran off to tell Jesus' friends.

Later Jesus' friends were in a room together.

Suddenly Jesus was with them too!

After just a few weeks,
Jesus was taken up to heaven.

At Easter we remember that Jesus died...

And that he is alive forever!

The Bible tells us God loved the people of this world so much that he gave Jesus to die for us so we never really die, but can live forever.